Division of Beat

A Breath Impulse Method For Intermediate Band Classes

BOOK 1B

Supplemental Material

Eastman Counting System...p. 33

Musical Terms.....................p. 34

By
Harry H. Haines
Music Department Chairman
West Texas State University
Canyon, Texas

And

J. R. McEntyre
Coordinator of Music
Odessa Public Schools
Odessa, Texas

Contributing Editor

Tom C. Rhodes

FINGERING CHART
TENOR SAXOPHONE

● —indicates hole closed (or key depressed).   ○ —indicates hole open.

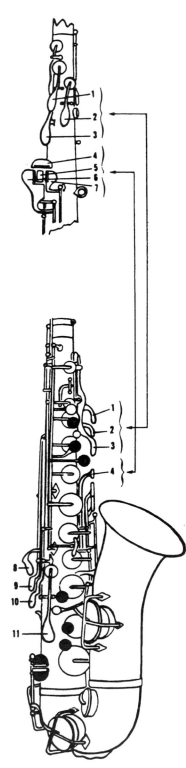

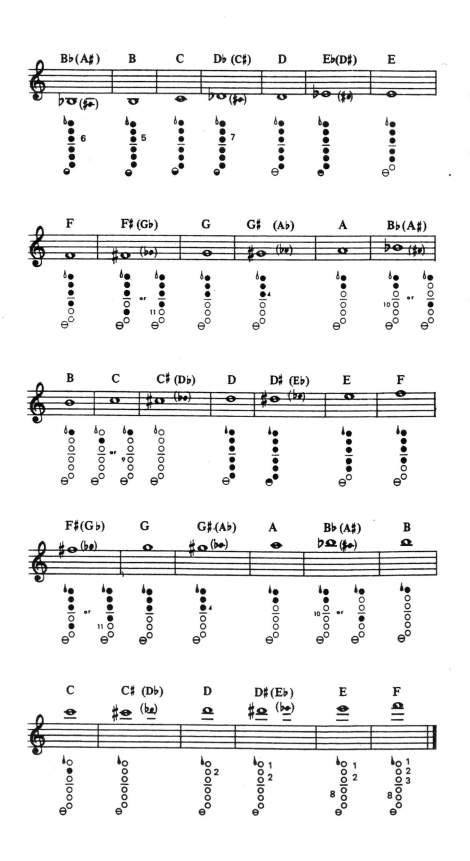

BAND WARM-UPS
To Be Added Gradually Throughout the Book

1 Two Breath Impulses Per Beat 4 breath impulses on each tone of the chromatic scale.

2 Three Breath Impulses Per Beat 6 breath impulses on each tone of the chromatic scale.

3 Four Breath Impulses Per Beat 8 breath impulses on each tone of the scale.

4 Six Breath Impulses Per Beat 12 breath impulses on each tone of the scale.

5 Eight-Five-One Slur Practice slowly! Work for smooth even slurs.

6 Flexibility Exercise Practice slowly at first, then push for greater speed.

7 Five-Note Slur Practice slowly (suggest $\quad$=50). Keep the airstream flowing smoothly! It's the *quality* of the slur that is most important.

8 Flexibility Exercise Practice slowly at first. If necessary, play each note as a ♪, then as a ♪.

B-378

LESSON I

1 Scale Partners

2 Duet Part

3 Chalumeau Etude

4 Slurring's the Thing

5 Chromatic Etude

Watch Out!

6 Amazing Grace

7 Grandfather's Clock

8 Little Canon

PART 2

PART 3

LESSON 2
Concert F Lesson

1 Scale Duo

2 Duet Part

3 Clarinets the Same (As Lesson One)

4 Chromatic Exercise

Watch out!

5 Skip To My Lou

6 Same Tune

7 Tom and Jerry Duet

8 Duet Part

LESSON 3

1. "The" Scale

2. Duet Part

3. Clarinets Right Hand Down

4. Chromatic Challenge

5. High School Cadets

6. Blue Bells of Scotland

7. Variation (Duet Part)

LESSON 4

Changing Keys

Partner Songs

B-378

Eighth, Quarter And Dotted-Quarter Rhythms

LESSON 5
The Dotted-Quarter-Note Lesson

1 Rhythmic Precision

2 Duet Part

3 Clarinets Help

4 Taps

5 Deck The Halls

6 All Through the Night

7 Dotted-Quarter Round

LESSON 6
More Dotted-Quarter Notes

1 Stay Together Duo

2 Duet Part

3 Chromatic Exercise   *Watch Out!*

4 Men of Harlech

5 Auld Lang Syne

6 Minor Melody

7 Accomp.

LESSON 7
The Syncopation Lesson

1 **Eighth Note Etude**

2 **Syn-Co-Pa Duo**

3 **Syncopated Chromatic**

Careful!

4 **Tom Dooley**

5 **Red River Valley**

6 **That's Where My Money Goes**

7 **You're A Grand Old Flag**

Cohan

LESSON 8
Harder Syncopation

1 Multiple Syncopation

2 Duet Part

3 Chromatic Syncopation - Watch Carefully!

4 Cindy

5 Old Gray Mare

6 John Henry *(Wait!)*

7 Hoky Poky

SIXTEENTH NOTE RHYTHMS
(To be played with 4 impulses per beat)

LESSON 9
Sixteenth Notes
(More 4 impulses per beat)

1 Rhythmic Scale

2 Part Two

3 Echo Song

4 Part Two

5 Music In The Air

6 Polly Wolly Doodle

7 Round: Frere Jacques

LESSON 10
(More 4 impulses per beat)

LESSON 11
The Enharmonic Lesson

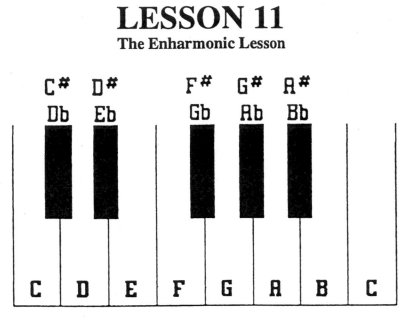

1 **Enharmonic Echo**

2 **Echo Part**

3 **Ascending And Descending Chromatic Scales**

4 **Song With Accidentals**

LESSON 12
The A-flat Concert Lesson

1 Our New Scale

2 Duet Part

3 Follow The Leader

4 Tutti

5 This Old Man

6 This New Man

7 American Patrol

8 Accomp.

DOTTED EIGHTH AND SIXTEENTH RHYTHMS

(To be played with 4 impulses per beat)

LESSON 13
Dotted-Eighth Lesson

1 Fun Dotted-Eighths

2 Duet Part

3 Dotted-Eighth Scale

4 Bride's Processional

5 O Christmas Tree

6 Processional

B-378

LESSON 14

1 **Rhythm Matching**

2 **Rhythm Matching Duet**

3 **Dotted Chromatic**

4 **Dotted-Eighth Processional**

5 **Duet Part**

6 **Rigoletto**

7 **Texas Song**

8 **Humoresque**

Partner Songs

9 **Swanee River**

LESSON 15

1 Dotted Scale

2 Dotted Duo

3 Duet Part

4 Railroad Song

5 March of the Kings

6 Santa Lucia

LESSON 16
More of the Same

1 Concert D-flat Scale Rhythm Practice

2 Air

3 Andante Duet

4 Duet Part

COMPOUND TIME RHYTHMS

Remember — the foot tap is "down-press-up"

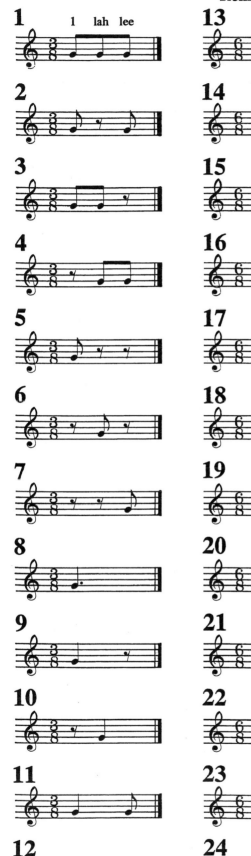

LESSON 17
The 3/8 Lesson

1 **Scale with Arpeggios**

2 **Part 2**

3 **Chromatic Scale in 3/8**

4 **Back Down Again**

5 **Good Morning to You**

6 **Halloween Song**

7 **Walking Down The Street**

LESSON 18
The 6/8 Lesson

1 Scale Rhythms

2 Duet Part

3 Over The River And Through The Woods

4 Three Blind Mice (Round)

5 Man On The Flying Trapeze
(In One)

LESSON 19

1 Chromatic Drill

2 Chromatic Speed Drill

3 For He's A Jolly Good Fellow

4 Drink To Me Only

5 Farmer In The Dell (Round)

6 Semper Fidelis

Sousa

7 Accomp.

LESSON 20

1 Scale in 9/8

2 Scale in 12/8

3 Morning Song

4 Sorcerer's Apprentice *(What is the last note of the 1st measure?)*

5 The Last Song

SUPPLEMENTARY LESSON I

1 Triplet Scale And Arpeggio

2 Chromatic Triplets

3 Etude

4 Beautiful Dreamer

5 Accomp.

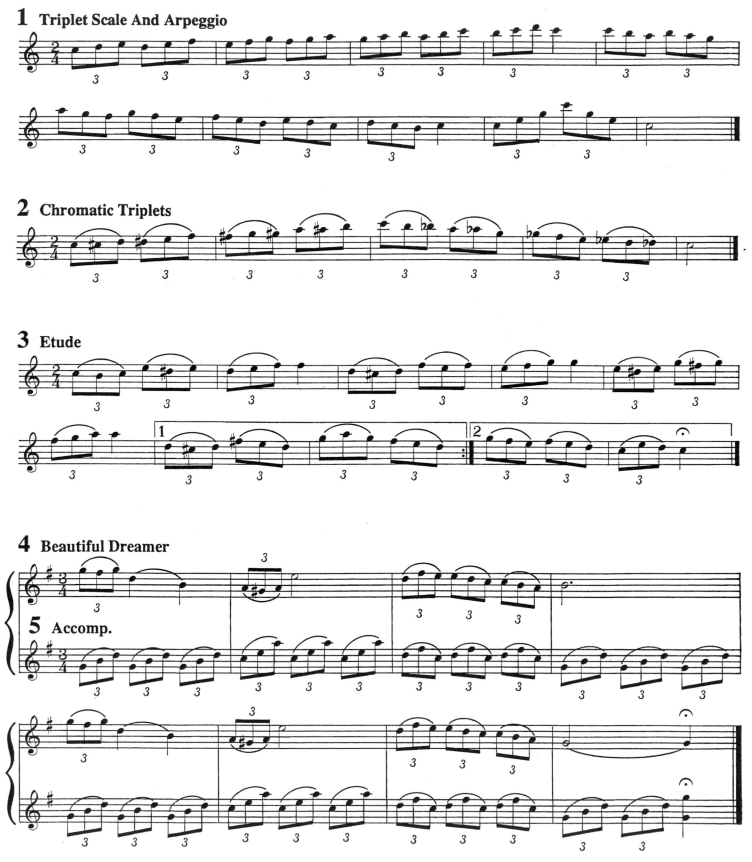

SUPPLEMENTARY LESSON II

(Extra Help To Get Ready For The Next Book)

B-378

Division of Beat

RHYTHM EXERCISES

Suggestion: For best results, use a metronome.

Set 1: The Blue and Green Slides

(All exercises on this page can be counted with 2 impulses)

*Exercises 73-84 should be counted one beat per measure using three pulses.
You could be tested on some of these rhythms.

Division of Beat

RHYTHM EXERCISES

Set 2: The Green and Red Slides

(For 3 impulses and 4 impulses)

Suggestion: For best results, use a metronome.

Division of Beat
RHYTHM EXERCISES

Set 3: The Yellow Slides
(for 6 impulses)

Suggestion: For best results, use a metronome when counting these rhythms.

*EASTMAN SYSTEM OF COUNTING (Simplified)

I. Notes of one or more counts

Notes of one count (or longer) are counted much the same way as any counting system; simply say the number of the count on which the note begins and continue the word-sound for the duration of the note. Thus a note which receives one count and which begins on the first beat of the measure would be counted "one"; if it were on the second count, say "two", etc. A note of longer value would simply be held longer; thus a whole note (in ₄ time) would be counted "onnnnnnnnnnne" for 4 counts. This has the advantage of making the verbalization most nearly approximate the sound of an instrument playing the actual rhythm and requires the identical mental process of thinking the number of counts while a continuous sound is produced. The following example quickly illustrates Eastman Counting as applied to rhythms (including rests) of 1, 2, 3 or 4 counts.

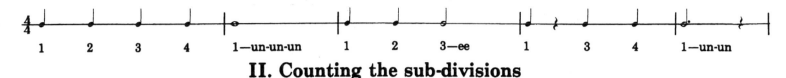

| 1 | 2 | 3 | 4 | 1—un-un-un | 1 | 2 | 3—ee | 1 | 3 | 4 | 1—un-un |

II. Counting the sub-divisions

Notes which receive less than a full count are divided into rhythms which are divisable by 2 and those which are divisable by 3 (some would say duple and triple rhythms). Again, any note which occurs on a downbeat is simply counted with the number of the count; the important difference is that a note which occurs the last ½ of a count is counted "te" (latin, rhymes with May) and notes which occur on the second ⅓ of the count and last ⅓ of the count are counted "lah" and "lee."

Rhythms which are divisable by 2

1   te

Rhythms which are divisable by 3

1   lah   lee

III. *Everything* else is counted "Ta"

1   ta   te   ta

1   te   ta

1   ta   te

1   ta

1   ta lah ta lee ta

1   lah ta lee ta

1   ta lah ta lee

1   ta lee

IV. Unusual counting situations

1. Two-beat triplet

4/4

1   lee   lah   3   lee   lah

2. 32nd Notes

2/4

1 ta ta ta te ta ta ta 2   te

3. Triplets in sub-division

3/8

1   ta ta lah   lee

4. When a measure contains beats of unequal duration, such as ⅝ or ⅞. Those beats with extra eighth notes are considered to have an extra "Te."

5/8   7/8

1 te 2 te te   1 te 2 te 3 te te

---

*For the complete explanation of this counting system, see *Ear Training and Sight Singing Dictation Manual* by Alan I. McHose, published by Prentice Hall.

MUSICAL TERMS, ABBREVIATIONS AND SIGNS

Accelerando—accel.	Gradually faster
Adagio	Slowly
Ad libitum	At liberty
Allargando	Louder and slower
Allegretto	Moderately fast; slower than *allegro*
Andantino	Faster than *andante*
Animato	With animation; with life
A tempo	In the original tempo
Cantabile	In a song-like style
Chromatic	Proceeding by half tones
Coda	The ending
Con brio	With spirit
Con moto	With motion
Crescendo—cresc.	Gradually louder
Da Capo—D.C.	Return to the beginning
Dal Segno—D.S.	From the sign
Decrescendo—decresc.	Gradually softer
Diminuendo—dim.	Gradually diminish sound
Dolce	Sweetly
Fine	The end
Forte—f	Loud
Fortissimo—ff	Very loud
Forzando—fz	With sudden emphasis
Giocoso	Humorously; playfully
Largo	The slowest tempo mark
Legato	In a smooth, connected style
Leggiero	Light; swift
Lento	Slowly, between *andante* and *largo*
L'istesso	In the same time or tempo
Ma non troppo	But not too much
Marcato	Marked; accented
Marcia	In a march style
Meno mosso	Less motion; slower
Mezzo piano—mp	Moderately soft
Mezzo forte—mf	Moderately loud
Moderato	Moderately
Molto	Very much
Morendo	Dying away
Pianissimo—pp	Very soft
Piano—p	Softly
poco a poco	Little by little
Presto	Very quick; faster than *allegro*
Rallentando—rall.	Gradually slower
Ritardando—rit.	Retarding; holding back
Ritenuto	Retarding; holding back
Simile	In the same manner
Sforzando—sfz	With emphasis on a single note or chord
Solo	For one performer
Soli	For all
Staccato	Separated; disconnected
Tutti	All; together
Valse	Waltz
Vivace	Lively; sprightly
𝄋	Sign
⊕	to *Coda*
⸺	*Crescendo*
⸺	*Decrescendo*
>	Accent

Selected Saxophone Music

ALL SAXOPHONES

Saxophone Etudes and Instruction

BAERMANN, CARL

Hite, David

B496   Foundation Studies   HL3770807
Based on the well-known studies of Carl Berarmann (Opus 63), this collection incorporates daily practice studies of scales, chords and intervals.

BARRETT, APOLLON

Hite, David

B381   40 Progressive Melodies   HL3770580

GEE, HARRY

B321   Progressive and Varied Etudes   HL3770445

HITE, DAVID

Hite, David

B379   Melodious and Progressive Studies, Bk. 1   HL3770578
This compilation is part of the established study repertoire for developing saxophone player/students. Includes: 18 Expressive Studies(scales)-Demnitz; 18 Expressive Studies (chords)-Demnitz; 9 Melodic Studies-Nocentini; 14 Melodic Etudes-Baermann; 5 Progressive Studies-Kayser and major and minor scales.

B472   Melodious and Progressive Studies, Bk. 2   HL3770715
This second volume of David Hite's Melodious and Progressive Studies has become part of the standard teaching repertoire for all saxophone player/students. It includes: 16 Caprices (Gambaro); 14 Etudes from Op. 37 (Dont); 6 Studies for the Development of the Tongue; 4 Expressive Studies; 3 Studies for Nimble Speed; 3 Chromatic Studies, 0 Studies for Flexibility, 2 Studies on Trills.

PARISI, STANISLAO

Gerardo Iasilli

B222   40 Technical and Melodious Studies, Bk. 1   HL3770305

ROSSARI, GUSTAVO

Gerardo Iasilli

B220   53 Melodious Etudes Bk 1   HL3770303
B221   53 Melodious Etudes, Bk. 2   HL3770304

ROUSSEAU, EUGENE

S150001   Saxophone High Tones   HL40163
A systematic approach to range extension for all saxophones.

S150008   Saxophone High Tones (Japanese Ed.)   HL40169
Translation by Atsuyasu Kitayama

TEAL, LARRY

S150004   Daily Studies for the Improvement of the   HL40166
           Saxophone Technique
Etudes for all saxophones

Saxophone Solo, unaccompanied

KARG-ELERT, SIGFRID

Jeffrey Lerner

B351   25 Caprices and an Atonal Sonata   HL3770521

KARG-ELERT, SIGFRID

Robert Ford

B487   23 Caprices   HL3770765

SOPRANO SAXOPHONE

Soprano Saxophone Solo with Keyboard

BACH, J.S.

Gee, Harry

SS882   Sonata No. 4 In C   HL3774559

HANDEL, GEORGE FRIDERIC

Gee, Harry

ST416   Adagio and Allegro   HL3775099

PIERNE, GABRIEL

Gee, Harry

SS906   Piece In G Minor   HL3774589

Soprano or Tenor Saxophone Solo with Keyboard

PLATTI, GIOVANNI

arr. Eugene Rousseau

S156001   Sonata in G   HL40201
Can also be performed with B-flat clarinet.

ALTO SAXOPHONE

Alto Saxophone Solo with Keyboard

BRAHMS, JOHANNES

arr. Eugene Rousseau

S151005   Sonata Op. 120 No. 1 in F minor   HL40172
Transcription of viola sonata.
S151007   Sonata Op. 120 No. 2 in E-flat major   HL40174
Transcription of clarinet sonata.

DEBUSSY, CLAUDE

arr. Eugene Rousseau

S151002   Rapsodie   HL40171
Rousseau brings to the Rapsodie an artistic sensibility--a fitting addition to the concert recital stage.

DEMERSSEMAN, JULES

Fred Hemke

ST520   Le Carnaval De Venise   HL3775239

HANDEL, GEORGE FRIDERIC

Gee, Harry

SS749   Adagio and Allegro   HL3774410

HEIDEN, BERNHARD

S151008   Diversion (piano reduction)   HL40175
Reduction of full wind ensemble version, available on rental.
S151009   Fantasia Concertante (piano reduction)   HL40176
Composed for Saxophone artist Eugene Rousseau.

Exclusively distributed by   HAL•LEONARD® CORPORATION

Questions/ comments? info@laurenkeisermusic.com

LOEILLET, JEAN BAPTISTE

Merriman, Lyle

SS886   Sonata   HL3774563

LUNDE, LAWSON

SS743   Sonata   HL3774405

REED, ALFRED

SS764   Ballade   HL3774427

SCHUMANN, ROBERT

Fred Hemke

ST38   Three Romances   HL3775044

STOCK, DAVID

X151020   Go for Two   HL116291

Go for Two for alto saxophone and piano consists of two contrasting movements: "Warmly" is a lyrical andante followed by a fast rhythmic second movement titled "Driving".

WARD, DAVID

SS101   An Abstract   HL3773701

TENOR SAXOPHONE

Tenor Saxophone Solo with Keyboard

ANDERSON, GARLAND

SS866   Sonata   HL3774544

HANDEL, GEORGE FRIDERIC

Arthur Ephross

ST342   Sonata No. 5 In E Flat   HL3774997

PASQUALE, JAMES DI

SS761   Sonata   HL3774424

SENAILLE, JEAN BAPTISTE

Arthur Ephross

ST361   Allegro Spiritoso   HL3775019

STEIN, LEON

SS864   Sonata   HL3774542

TUTHILL, BURNET

SS867   Sonata   HL3774545

BARITONE SAXOPHONE

Baritone Saxophone Solo, unaccompanied

BACH, J.S.

Kasprzyk, James

SS763   Suite No. 1   HL3774426

SS904   Suite No. 4   HL3774587

Baritone Saxophone Solo with Keyboard

ANDERSON, GARLAND

ST172   Sonata   HL3774770

DAVIS, WILLIAM MAC

ST442   Variations On a Theme of Robert   HL3775129
        Schumann

SENAILLE, JEAN BAPTISTE

Gee, Harry

ST20   Allegro Spiritoso   HL3774802

SPEARS, JARED

ST308   Ritual and Celebration   HL3774951

SAXOPHONE DUO

Unaccompanied

TULL, FISHER

ST752   Dialogue   HL3775558

SAXOPHONE ENSEMBLES

Saxophone Trio

BEETHOVEN, LUDWIG VAN

arr. Larry Teal

S153002   Trio Op. 87 (SAT or ATB)   HL40183

A staple in the repertory of saxophone chamber music transcriptions.

HOOK, JAMES

Gee, Harry

SS897   Adagio and Allegretto   HL3774579

ROSSI, SALAMONE

Himie Voxman/ R.p. Block

ST468   Three Canzonets   HL3775165

Saxophone Quartet (SATB)

MOSZKOWSKI, MORITZ

arr. Michael Cunningham

X154012   Italian Serenade "Guitarre"   HL42665

Transcribed from Moszkowski's "Guitar" Serenade Op. 45 No. 2.

QUARTETS, MIXED

Saxophone

HARTLEY, WALTER

SU410   Trio Concertino   HL3776320

Dedicated to the Lexington Trio, Walter Hartley's Concertino is among the prolific composer's most performed works. Versions for trio accompanied by both piano and band are available from the publisher. Duration ca. 9'.

Exclusively distributed by  HAL•LEONARD® CORPORATION

Questions/ comments? info@laurenkeisermusic.com